BIRMINGHAM CITY
University

Featherstone

as for
play

...GHAM AND SALLY FEATHERSTONE

Featherstone
An imprint of Bloomsbury Publishing Plc

50 Bedford Square
London
WC1B 3DP
UK

1385 Broadway
New York
NY 10018
USA

www.bloomsbury.com

Bloomsbury is a registered trademark of Bloomsbury Publishing Plc

First published 2016

Text © Phill and Sally Featherstone, 2016

Photographs © Phill and Sally Featherstone/ © Shutterstock/ © LEYF

British Library Cataloguing-in-Publication Data
A catalogue record for this book is available from the British Library.

ISBN:
PB 978-1-4729-1914-4
ePDF 978-1-4729-1915-1

Library of Congress Cataloging-in-Publication Data
A catalogue record for this book is available from the Library of Congress.

10 9 8 7 6 5 4 3 2 1

Printed in Great Britain by Ashford Colour Press Ltd

This book is produced using paper that is made from wood grown in managed, sustainable
forests. It is natural, renewable and recyclable. The logging and manufacturing processes
conform to the environmental regulations of the country of origin.

To view more of our titles please visit www.bloomsbury.com

Contents

Introduction

Most children love messy activities, particularly those involving slime, ooze, gloop, mud, found materials and water, often in imaginative combinations. These are the stuff of play for every child, and should be valued for their contribution to childhood memories, as well as providing a foundation for future learning in mathematics, science, language, problem solving and for making friends. We could easily fill a book with memorable everyday experiences such as riding bikes through paint, stamping in puddles, picking up handfuls of mud, using a swing for an alternative purpose, or throwing a wet ball at a wall. Children do these things independently every day in the best settings, where their explorations are valued.

However, we know that practitioners are always on the lookout for new activities or ingredients, or old activities with a new twist, and in this book we have tried to give you 50 ways to offer messy play that you may not have used yet (or perhaps have forgotten that you enjoyed before).

Nowadays every activity must have a purpose, and practitioners need to be able to explain why messy and fleeting experiences are still important. Managers and parents are often particularly concerned about messy play, and ask what the benefits are of activities with no 'end result'. There can be an over emphasis on results to be measured, rather than on processes which have no lasting outcome and are 'merely' enjoyed. It is important to ensure that these activities are available to every child, and that we know why we are offering them!

Here's why we think messy play is important:

- Listening and attention: in order to follow the activities in these pages children will need to listen attentively in a range of situations, to the adults with them and to each other.

- Understanding: children will need to follow instructions involving several ideas or actions, and be able to answer 'how' and 'why' questions about their experiences.

- Speaking: children will talk about what's happening in a range of situations, using words to describe – and in some cases explain – what they see, hear and feel.

- Moving and handling: many of the activities require control and coordination in large and small movements. The demands made on hands, arms and fingers will stimulate the muscular development and control needed for writing.

- Health and self-care: it's vital for children to learn how to handle things safely, looking after themselves and each other. There's detailed health and safety advice for adults within the activity pages, but children should be constantly reminded of the importance of thinking about what's going on and taking care.

- Self-confidence and self-awareness: the activities will help children develop the confidence to try new activities, and to say why they like some more than others. They will be encouraged to say when they do or don't need help.

- Managing feelings and behaviour: some of these activities won't work unless children collaborate, following the simple rules they're given. If an activity doesn't work, there's the chance to talk about the reasons why, and to learn how to handle disappointment as well as celebrate success.

- Exploring and using media and materials: children will probably have encountered some of the materials featured, but many will be new. The messy activities give them the chance to explore and experiment with colours, shapes, textures, forms and functions, by exploring the materials for their unique qualities, not always expecting a finished 'end result'.

- Being imaginative and creative: predicting and then observing what happens will give children the chance to use what they already know about media and materials, to take on new ideas and experiences and to express themselves creatively, in language and physically.

Using this book

The pages are all organised in the same way. Before you start any activity we suggest you read everything on the page.

What you need lists the resources required for the activity, and usually for the suggested extensions too. These are basic, and are likely to be already available in most settings or can be bought in a shop or on the internet. Where less usual items appear we've tried to suggest sources. We recommend that you check this list before embarking on any activity with the children, as well as reading about how they are used.

Top tips give a brief suggestion or piece of advice to help in tackling the activity – these are things we wish we had known before we did them!

What to do tells you step-by-step how to complete the activity. There are sometimes internet references relevant to the instructions we have given. All the sites quoted were active and available at the time of writing, but the internet is constantly changing so we can't guarantee they'll always be there.

Taking it forward gives ideas for additional activities, or for developing the activity further. These will be particularly useful for things that have gone especially well or where children show a real interest. In many cases they use the same resources, and in every case they have been designed to extend learning and broaden the children's experiences.

The **Health & Safety** tips are often obvious, but safety can't be overstressed. In most cases there are no specific hazards involved, and your usual health and safety measures should be enough. In others there are particular issues to be noted and addressed.

Finally, **What's in it for the children?** tells you (and others) briefly how the suggested activities contribute to learning.

Preparation

We've tried out all these activities ourselves, and we learnt more about exactly how they work by doing them. So we suggest that you have a go yourself before trying them with children. It will help you see what's involved, anticipate any problems and how your children will respond.

Health & Safety

The idea is that most children should do most of what's in these pages themselves. However, some of the activities need an adult to take over some aspects if they are to be completed safely. For example, anything that involves handling hot items or substances, or using sharp knives. Generally these are pointed out in the text, but we rely on the expertise of the practitioner to ensure that tasks are done without risk.

None of the suggested activities use ingredients that are harmful, but only one activity (Eat a monster, page 60) is actually edible. This is important, because some of the finished results look and smell inviting. Warn children against tasting, and try to discourage any finger lickers.

Be aware that some children may have allergic reactions to some substances. We've tried to point out where these might occur, but we recommend that you regularly check on allergies in your group, and keep a list of these in a prominent place in your room.

On one page (Big tie dye, page 63) we suggest that the children use protective gloves. There may be other places where you're tempted to use these, but we think you should avoid them unless you consider them absolutely necessary, or an individual child has a skin problem or allergy. Touching and feeling the materials is an essential part of the experience.

One activity (Snow gak, page 34) requires borax. This is perfectly safe if handled properly.

Sand foam

A new take on an old favourite

What you need:

- A small bucket of sand
- A can of shaving foam
- An empty water tray or plastic storage box

Top tip ⭐

The children can do this activity independently if they particularly love squirting the foam!

Taking it forward

- Make bubbling quicksand: mix three cups of sand with two cups of cornflour, two cups of bicarbonate of soda and two cups of warm water. Spread your mixture in the bottom of a shallow tray and add some spoons and scoops. Play with this cornflour mix, then let the children squirt vinegar onto it from spray bottles. The sand will bubble and fizz.

What's in it for the children?

Different ways of using familiar substances such as sand will encourage children to explore tactile materials and use their hand and finger muscles.

✚ Health & Safety

Make sure the shaving foam is non-allergenic and fragrance free.

What to do:

1. Pour the sand into a pile in your tray.
2. Spread it out in a thick layer.
3. Spray the foam all over the top of the sand.
4. Work the foam into the sand by squeezing and kneading it until it is soft and gloopy.
5. Use this foam without tools, to squidge and pour from hand to hand.
6. If children's interest wanes, tip the foam into a builder's tray and let the children walk in it, either barefoot or with boots on.

Spray away
Spraying over shapes

What you need:

- A roll of lining paper or thick wallpaper
- Thin ready-mixed paint in several colours
- Clean plastic sprays (garden hand sprays are ideal)
- A collection of objects from indoors and outside
- Big wooden bricks or stones to hold the paper down
- A sheltered spot in your garden or outdoor area

Top tip ⭐

This is best done outside, on a fine, still day.

Taking it forward

- When your creation is dry, try putting all the objects back in the right places.
- Some of the oldest pictures in the world are hand sprays on cave walls. See if you can find some examples on the internet, then try your own version on paper fixed to an outside wall.

What's in it for the children?

This activity gives children practice in working together, and making something that could be used as a display for their room.

✚ Health & Safety

Don't spray directly at other people!

What to do:

1. Pour some water into the spray bottles.
2. Show the children the spray bottles, and talk about where they can and can't spray. Then let them try 'free spraying' with water, preferably outside.
3. When the children have tried free spraying, refill the spray bottles with paint.
4. Put a length of paper on the ground and hold it down with stones, bricks or paint.
5. Let the children spread the objects you have collected on the paper. Larger objects, with clear outlines work better.
6. Now spray the paint all over the paper, using different colours. Several children can spray at once, so you may need to help with negotiation.
7. Leave the paint to dry for a bit, then remove the objects to see how they have left their mark.
8. Roll out some more paper and let the children collect some more objects to spray. You could try natural objects such as leaves, sticks, stones and flowers.

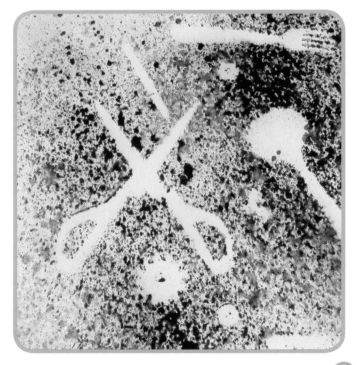

Swirly whirly

Take prints from cornflour gloop

What you need:

- Two cups cornflour
- Two cups water
- Measuring cup
- Plastic trays
- **Food colourings** (red, green and blue, but use more if you like)
- White paper

Top tip ⭐

Clean cat litter trays are great for all sorts of messy play.

What to do:

1. Help the children to make enough gloop for the group, by mixing cornflour and water in a ratio of two measures of cornflour to one of water. Mix it in one or more trays – more trays enable more children to join in.

2. Play with the gloop. The children can squeeze it and stir it with their hands.

3. Leave it for a moment and see how it goes from liquid to solid and back again.

4. Add just a few drops of one of the food colourings to the gloop. Swirl it into the mixture with your fingers.

5. Add another colour, and swirl again.

6. Add a third colour and swirl some more. Pull the colour into shapes. Watch and talk about the colours and patterns.

7. Lay a sheet of white paper on the surface of the gloop and press it down gently. Lift the paper off to make a print of the swirly pattern.

Taking it forward

- Take some digital photos of your gloop patterns. Download and print them to make pictures for the wall and for greeting cards.

- Squirt some shaving foam into the tray, add some more food colours and try some more swirling.

What's in it for the children?

This activity encourages children to experiment and talk about what they find.

Cloud dough

A simple, soft water-free dough

What you need:

- A big mixing bowl
- Measuring cup
- Eight cups of plain flour
- One cup cooking oil (preferably vegetable or plant based)
- Food colouring
- Small plastic cake moulds, bun tins, paper cake cases
- Plastic spoons, butter knives, small rolling pins
- Small boards

Top tip ⭐

Store some of the un-coloured dough in a large ziplock bag or sealed container to come back to later. If unused, it'll keep for months.

Taking it forward

- Try using perfumed baby oil, or adding a little lavender oil, to scent your dough.

- Mix in some glow-in-the-dark paint, put the activity in a dark place, then shine a black light torch on it. You can get the paint and the torch from Amazon.

What's in it for the children?

Modelling and moulding develops gross and fine motor skills.

➕ **Health & Safety**

Take extra care if you offer the children tools with points or sharp edges.

What to do:

1. Help the children to measure eight cups of flour into a big bowl.

2. Make a crater in the middle of the flour and add one cup of oil.

3. Mix it up thoroughly by hand until the dough holds together when squeezed. Add a little more oil or flour until you're happy with the consistency. The mix should be soft and easy to mould, but not too wet or oily. Try to get rid of any big lumps of flour.

4. This dough will hold together when pressed, but falls apart again like damp sand when you let go – it does not need water!

5. Experiment with the dough. Make shapes, worms, flowers or animals. Make 'dough pies' with all sorts of moulds.

6. Put some of the dough in another container and add food colouring, then experiment some more.

7. Take handprints or prints of other objects. Use the cases and tins to make pretend cakes, and decorate these with buttons, beads or glitter.

8. Roll out the dough and make some impressions using small objects: Lego™ bricks, coins and combs work well, but there are plenty of other options.

Swings and slides

Use your swings and slide for painting

What you need:

- A collection of mark makers – sponges, all sorts of brushes and kitchen cleaners, rollers, bath scrunchies, feather dusters, balls of all sorts
- Ready-mixed paint
- Bowls
- Spoons
- Decorator's paintbrushes
- Lots of string and elastic
- A place outside to hang objects on strings
- Lining paper on a roll
- Masking tape
- Bricks or logs to hold the paper down

Top tip ★

Buy lining paper or rolls of wallpaper from a DIY shop - it's cheaper than display paper.

What to do:

1. Find a horizontal bar or branch to hang the objects on – a climbing frame, swing frame, shed doorway or tree branch would work well. Make sure there is room for the painted objects to swing.

2. Tie some strings from the horizontal bar, tie a length of elastic on the end of each string, then tie objects on the elastics, checking that the objects just touch the ground.

3. Roll some paper out under the objects.

4. Roll some paper down your slide, and fix it in place with masking tape.

5. Pour some paint into bowls, cups or foil dishes, checking that it is quite runny. Let the children choose whether to work on the slide or the swinging brushes.

On the slide

6. Choose a colour of paint and drip it onto the paper on the slide, so it runs down. They can take a pot and brush to the top of the slide, or stand on the ground and reach up. You may need to help!

7. Drip paint at the top of the slide and watch what happens. As more paint reaches the slope, it should start to run down to the bottom, creating paths as it drips.

8. Keep dripping and dropping different colours to make patterns.

On the strings

9. Hold a paint dish in one hand and dip one of the objects into the paint.

10. Now find some different ways to make the objects make marks on the paper – swinging, bouncing, throwing, 'pinging' to make patterns on the paper. Pour some paint on the paper if this helps.

11. Encourage the children to keep experimenting with the activity. They could prop up the paper, make the strings longer or shorter, or drip and roll paint from brushes and bowls.

Taking it forward

- Tie strings round children's wrists and fingers and fix balls, sponges and brushes to the ends of these. Bounce the objects along the paper, making prints and patterns.

- Send some cars or painted table tennis balls down the slide and look at the patterns and markings they make.

What's in it for the children?

Working together in play situations improves children's social skills.

Health & Safety

Strings and elastic can get tangled round necks and limbs, so be vigilant!

50 fantastic ideas for messy play

Ice age rescue

Release them from the ice!

What you need:

- Small plastic animals and small world people, such as Lego® figures
- A plastic container for each one or two figures (plastic storage boxes, family size yoghurt or cream pots)
- Three or four squirt bottles filled with strongly coloured water
- A bowl of salt
- A teaspoon
- A large plastic storage box, builder's tray or empty sand/water tray
- Hammer and screwdriver (for older children)

Top tip ⭐

Children particularly enjoy this activity, so have another set of animals and ice blocks ready if needed, or repeat the activity the next day.

Taking it forward

- Freeze other small figures in ice and float them in your water tray.

What's in it for the children?

This is a problem-solving activity, and involves thinking skills as well as fine and gross motor skills.

✚ Health & Safety

When you offer tools, train the children to use them properly. If you are worried, use child-sized metal spoons and forks instead.

What to do:

This should be done in two parts.

Day 1:

1. Put one or two of the animals in each of the plastic pots. Let the children fill the containers with water and put them in the freezer.

Day 2 (or when thoroughly frozen):

2. Tip the ice out of the pots into the large storage box.

3. Make up a story together about animals and people who are trapped in the ice. The animals and people need to be rescued – can the children rescue them?

4. Show the children the coloured water, the salt, the hammer and the screwdriver and ask them to predict which they think will work best to release the figures.

5. The children will probably suggest the hammer and the screwdriver first, but will need to take care not to 'hurt' the animals and people in the blocks. Help them to try this method (watch out for ice splinters). This method will almost certainly prove to be difficult and dangerous, especially for the figures in the ice!

6. Some children may now suggest using the salt. Try this together, pouring the salt onto the ice with the spoons and watching what happens. The salt will begin to melt the ice.

7. However, a combination of salt and spraying with the coloured water will work better than either of the previous methods, and in time they should be able to get all the animals free.

floating foam

What you need:

- A can of shaving foam
- A big bowl, plastic storage box or water tray
- Ready-mixed paint or food colouring
- Plastic pipettes or droppers

Top tip ⭐

Put the tray on a firm surface so the water doesn't slop about.

What to do:

1. Put about 6cm of cold water in your container.
2. Let the children spray the shaving foam all over the surface of the water in patterns, lines and squiggles – it will float.
3. Play with the white foam.
4. Colour this lovely fluffy stuff by using the pipettes to drip paint or food colouring.
5. Now swirl and swish the foam with fingers, hands, sticks, or other objects to make swirly patterns.
6. Pile the coloured foam in heaps, try to push it under the water (it won't sink).
7. When the foam starts to disintegrate, tip it out and do it all again.

Taking it forward

- Try some marbling by mixing oil and paint. Drop this mixture onto water and swirl it gently. Take some prints of the patterns.

What's in it for the children?

This early science experiment is a great one for beginning to explore floating and sinking.

✚ Health & Safety

Use non-allergenic shaving foam.

The painted den
Make your own hideout

What you need:

- **A large sheet of fabric** (an old curtain, sheet, shower curtain, or tablecloth)
- **Hammer and nails, or duct tape**
- **Paint**
- **PVA glue**
- **Bowls or foil dishes**
- **Brushes, sponges and other painting implements**
- **Rope**
- **Clothes pegs**
- **Big bricks, logs or big stones**

Top tip ⭐

Fix a wooden batten and some sturdy hooks into the wall outside, so you can fix paper or fabric easily and quickly for outdoor creative activities.

Taking it forward

- Provide canes, cable ties, plastic sheet or sheer fabrics for regular den making.
- If you have a huge box or packaging from a fridge or washing machine, make this into a den by cutting doors and windows in it, and painting it inside and out.

What's in it for the children?

This activity is completely child-led, and leaves children free to express themselves and use their whole bodies.

✚ Health & Safety

Messy play outside always needs special attention as children tend to be much more lively and active out of doors!

What to do:

1. Collect everything you need and take it into your garden or outdoor area.

2. Fix your fabric to the wall, the side of a shed, or a fence. If you haven't got a vertical space, put the fabric on the ground and work flat, but the activity is much more fun on a vertical surface.

3. Pour some paint in trays or dishes – add enough water to make it fairly runny for splashing and splattering. If you put some PVA glue in the paint, it will make the den a bit more resistant to rain.

4. Put all the brushes and other implements next to the paint.

5. You may need to show the children what to do, but most of them will instinctively be able to use the paint in imaginative ways, splashing, flicking, splodging, throwing. This activity has few limits, except that the paint must go in the direction of the fabric!

6. Stay near, and provide more paint when needed.

7. When the children have finished, and this may take some time, leave the fabric to dry on the wall before the next stage.

8. When the paint is dry, tie a rope between two sturdy points in your area. These could be between the legs of a climbing frame, between two trees, from the railings to a hook in the wall, from two hooks fixed so the rope goes across a corner of your area.

9. Hang your fabric over the rope, so the ends are on the ground, and use clothes pegs to keep the fabric in place. Put logs, stones or bricks on the edges of the fabric to hold the den open.

10. Collect some cushions, a sleeping bag, some soft toys or a basket of books to put inside your painted den.

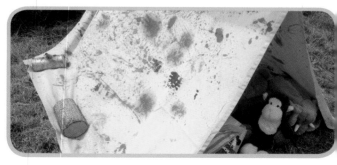

Going on a googly hunt

A pure white dough with a difference

What you need:

- Two cups hair conditioner
- Four cups cornflour
- A big bowl
- A wooden spoon
- Food colouring
- Googly eyes
- Aromatherapy oils (optional)
- Glitter (optional)

Top tip ⭐

The cheapest hair conditioner is fine for this activity.

Taking it forward

- Hide other things in the slime – small plastic animals, buttons, coins, marbles or small plastic letters. The children feel for them and try to identify and describe them from touch alone.

What's in it for the children?

Stirring and kneading develop arm muscles and motor skills essential for writing. Adding perfume always enhances learning.

➕ **Health & Safety**

Hair conditioners are safe but, as always, be aware of allergies, and choose a product that is non-allergenic.

What to do:

This is a very simple activity - let the children do it independently.

1. Mix the first two ingredients in a one:two ratio – one cup of hair conditioner to two cups of cornflour. If you want a bigger quantity, just double or treble the amounts as appropriate.

2. Stir the mixture thoroughly.

3. The dough should be smooth, silky and pure white. If it's crumbly add a little more conditioner. If it's too damp add a little more cornflour. Keep tweaking until the consistency feels right (the children can decide this).

4. You can add some food colouring if you like, but the pure white dough is lovely as it is.

5. Let the children play with the dough for a while before you move on to the next stage.

6. Scoop the dough into a deep sided plastic container.

7. Let some of the children hide the googly eyes for others to find.

Stamp piggy stamp
Make splashy pink pictures

What you need:

- A balloon pump
- **Balloons** (small ones are easier to handle)
- Pink paint
- PVA glue
- Plates or flat tins
- Buttons
- Googly eyes
- Big sheets of paper
- A bucket or big bowl

What to do:

1. Mix some pink paint with a little PVA glue, and pour it into shallow containers.
2. Blow up a balloon for each child and tie the ends. Don't blow the balloons up too big – they will print better if they are a bit squashy.
3. Show the children how to dip their balloons in the paint and stamp them on the paper to make pink circles.
4. Stamp balloon circles all over the paper.
5. Put the paint-covered balloons in a bucket!
6. Now dip your finger in the paint and make fingerprints on both sides of the top of each circle to create ears.
7. Stick some googly eyes on the wet paint.
8. Stick a button nose in place on the wet paint. Re-dip your finger in paint to use as glue if required. Once dry, display the pig pictures in your setting.

Top tip ⭐

This activity is great if the children all print together on one big piece of paper, either on the floor or on a big table.

Taking it forward

- Use the squishy balloons outside with water or thin paint, to make squishy prints on walls and paving stones.
- Use the same technique to make animal prints of cats with black paint, monkeys with brown paint, or even children.

What's in it for the children?

This activity is good for children who have not yet developed a good hand grasp or grip.

✚ Health & Safety

Be aware that some children are really scared of balloons. Softer balloons are less likely to pop! Balloons can be a choking hazard. Don't let children put them in their mouths or try to blow them up.

That's CnDice!
Painting with ice cubes

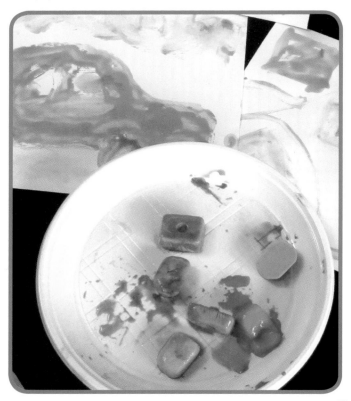

What you need:

- Cup measure
- Four cups cornflour
- Three to four cups water
- Ready-mixed paint or food colouring in several colours
- Small bowls
- Small cups or jugs for pouring the mixture
- Spoons
- Ice cube trays
- Lolly sticks or craft sticks (optional)
- Thick paper
- Cooking oil and thick brushes

What to do:

Day 1

1. Mix the cornflour with enough water to make a runny mixture.

2. Tip the mixture into several different containers and add paint or food colouring to each. Stir gently.

3. Pour the mixture carefully into the ice cube trays, add a lolly stick to each, and freeze overnight.

Day 2

4. Remove the ice cube trays from the freezer.

5. Tip the ice chalk out of the trays into bowls or plates, and let the children use them for drawing.

6. Take another piece of paper and coat it thinly with oil, using a thick brush.

7. Draw again and watch what happens to the paint on the paper as the ice cubes melt.

Top tip ⭐

The lolly sticks are optional, but some children may get cold fingers without them.

Taking it forward

- Make giant paint-coloured ice cubes in plastic food containers. Put some paper (thick lining paper or reversed wallpaper) in the bottom of an empty water tray, and tip the big ice cubes out onto the paper. Shunt the ice cubes around to make patterns on the paper.

What's in it for the children?

Watching changes happen to familiar materials, such as flour and water, is an early chemistry experience.

✚ Health & Safety

Just because they may look like lollies doesn't mean they're good to eat!

Slippery soap
Soap flake slime

What you need:

- **Box of soap flakes** ('liquid soap flakes' do not work for this activity)
- **Four to five jugs of warm water**
- **Powder paint, water based paint or liquid food colouring in various colours**
- **A variety of whisks** (including an old-fashioned rotary whisk, if you have one), **plastic cutlery and kitchen implements**
- **A bucket or bowl**
- **A builder's tray or other big container**

What to do:

Day 1

1. Tip the soap flakes into the bowl or bucket.

2. Pour in the warm water (it needs to be at least as hot as children's bath water in order to dissolve the flakes properly).

3. Let the children help you to make sure the mixture is thoroughly mixed, using their hands.

4. Leave this mixture in the bucket overnight. It will set into a soft, rubbery lump.

Top tip ★

Find cheap soap flakes in bargain stores or online, or make your own by grating bars of soap with a cheese grater.

Day 2

5. Tip the mixture into a builder's tray and add whisks, plastic cutlery, potato mashers and other kitchen implements.

6. Let the children explore the soap flake slab with the tools and see what happens – the lump will break down into soft pieces.

7. Offer the children some water so they can turn the mixture into soap slime again. They can try different tools, and see which works best.

8. It will take time to get the mixture fully dissolved in the water, but it will go back into slime – a gooey, squidgy, smooth paste.

9. Give the children plenty of time to squeeze and feel the paste.

10. Add some paint or food colouring to the soapy base. Whisk in the colours and watch them make marbled patterns and whirls.

11. Dilute the mixture further with warm water, and offer whisks, small bowls, cups and scoops to make and play with lots of bubbles.

12. Talk about how the slime feels, smells and looks. Encourage the children to use descriptive vocabulary: squidgy, slimy, gloopy, etc.

Taking it forward

- Make a cheaper version of soapy bubbles by soaking some bargain bars of soap in warm water overnight in a bowl or deep tray. In the morning let the children squeeze and squidge the bars until they dissolve (add some more warm water if you need it). When the soap has completely dissolved, use whisks to make lots of bubbles, and colour these with food colouring if you like.

What's in it for the children?

Using the whisks needs coordination, hand strength and thinking skills. The whisks (especially a rotary one) offer opportunities for developing both gross and fine motor skills.

✚ Health & Safety

There are likely to be spills and the soap will make surfaces slippery. Make sure you supervise these activities carefully.

Sizzling snowballs!

Frozen erupting dough

What you need:

- Cup measure
- Two cups bicarbonate of soda (baking soda)
- One cup of cornflour
- One and a quarter cups of warm water
- Food colouring
- Saucepan, wooden spoon
- Vinegar
- Plastic squeezy bottles
- Baking sheet or tray

Top tip ⭐

This dough will keep well in an airtight tin or a ziplock bag.

Taking it forward

- Make some fizzing cups by mixing food colouring, baking soda and cornflour with plenty of water and pour into small plastic cups. Drop vinegar into the cups from a pipette and see what happens.

What's in it for the children?

The fizzing excitement of these activities is fun, and helps children to observe changes in materials.

➕ Health & Safety

Wash your hands thoroughly after playing with baking soda mixtures, and rub in a little moisturiser. Salt will dry out the skin.

What to do:

1. Combine the baking soda, cornflour, food colouring and water in a saucepan. Mix well with the wooden spoon.

2. Heat on medium heat (adult only).

3. Constantly stir the ingredients until the mixture boils and begins to thicken. This will take several minutes.

4. When the mixture starts to come together and looks like mashed potatoes, scoop it out onto a tray or plastic mat to cool down. Cover it with a damp cloth.

5. Once the dough is cool enough to handle, knead it until it is smooth and sticks together.

6. Play with the dough for a bit, so it is really well mixed.

7. Make some balls about the size of marbles.

8. Leave the tray of balls to dry in a warm place for a couple of hours.

9. When the balls are dry, tip them onto a plastic plate.

10. Put some vinegar in the squeezy bottles and tighten the tops securely.

11. Squirt the vinegar onto the snowballs and watch what happens.

Hot rocks
A new use for old crayons

What you need:

- Large, smooth stones – at least one per child
- Kitchen foil
- Baking trays
- Small bowls – one for each stone
- Old flannels
- Oven mitts or kitchen tongs
- Wax crayons

Top tip ⭐

If you collect stones from outside, leave them overnight in water with a few drops of bleach, then dry before using.

Taking it forward

- Let the children break up some old crayons and put them in an old bun tin. Put in a low oven till they're melted. When they are cool the children can use them to draw with. Admire and talk about the swirly colours.

- Use your painted stones to make a brightly coloured rock-scape for play people.

What's in it for the children?

Predicting what will happen is a good learning exercise. Melting liquids and solids is part of early science.

➕ Health & Safety

This activity uses hot objects and needs close adult supervision. Don't tackle it without being sure you have enough adults to watch all the children closely.

What to do:

1. Place the dry stones on baking trays.
2. This next step is for adults only. Heat the oven to 100°C (gas mark ½).
3. Put the tray of stones in the oven.
4. Line the bowls with foil and sit each bowl on a flannel to steady it.
5. Peel most of the paper off the crayons.
6. Take the stones out of the oven (adult only) and, using mitts or tongs put one in each bowl. Wait till they're still hot but touchable. Don't guess – try each one, they may cool at different rates.
7. Warn the children that the stones are still hot. Show them the crayons and invite them to decorate the stone with blobs, squiggles and lines. The crayons should melt as they touch the stones.
8. You might want to put all or some of the stones back in the oven for another warming to see what happens, or to warm them up for more colours. (Optional, and for adults only).

Streeeeetch
Stretchy, black, sparkly dough

What you need:

- Cup and spoon measures
- One cup of slightly diluted black paint
- One teaspoon gelatine
- One tablespoon vegetable oil
- One cup flour
- Two teaspoons cream of tartar
- Third of a cup of salt
- Generous amounts of glitter
- An old saucepan
- A wooden spoon

What to do:

1. Pour the cup of paint into a medium saucepan, and sprinkle the gelatine powder over the top. (Adult only).

2. Turn the burner to medium and stir the liquid for a few minutes until the gelatine is dissolved.

3. Turn the heat down while you mix in all the other ingredients, except the glitter, and then turn the heat back up to medium.

4. Stir constantly until the dough thickens and begins to form a large clump around the spoon (this should only take about a minute).

5. At this point, remove from heat and turn the dough out onto a plate or greaseproof paper to cool.

6. Once it's completely cool, knead the dough until it is soft and stretchy, mixing in plenty of glitter as you knead.

Top tip ⭐

Buy glitter and food colouring in bulk - it's much cheaper.

Taking it forward

- Make glitterslime with half a cup each of PVA glue and liquid starch. Mix them up until you have a good pile of slime. Colour it with food colouring and add some glitter.

- Make stretchy chocolate dough! Replace the black paint with brown paint, and add some cocoa powder. Remind the children not to eat it!

What's in it for the children?

Any malleable activity that involves kneading and pummelling exercises hands and fingers for writing and other fine motor skills.

✚ Health & Safety

Keep the children away from hot surfaces and don't let them handle the dough until it has cooled.

Magic sprinkles
Salt sprinkles on ice

What you need:

- Small plastic containers – the number and size will depend on how much room you have in your freezer
- Shallow plastic trays or an empty sand or water tray
- Salt in a squeezy bottle
- Liquid watercolour paint, or food colouring
- Droppers or plastic pipettes (one for each colour)

Top tip ⭐

Put small amounts of salt out at a time, or it will all go at once! This is a good activity to do outside on a cold day.

Taking it forward

- You can keep the finished blocks in a freezer to look at again and talk about. Make a record over time with your camera. Watching the blocks dissolve encourages observation and concentration.
- Try some containers of different sizes and shapes – bowls, trays, deep and shallow pots.

What's in it for the children?

Talking with the children about exactly what's happening with the ice, salt and paint introduces some scientific concepts and early scientific language.

✚ Health & Safety

Fingers may get cold, so the children may need gloves.

What to do:

Day 1

1. Fill the containers with water and put them in the freezer till the water has turned into solid ice.

Day 2

2. Put the ice blocks in the plastic trays.
3. Sprinkle a little salt over the top surface of each ice block.
4. Watch what the salt does to the ice. Leave it for a minute or two so it begins to melt.
5. Using the droppers, drip the colouring on to the ice, a drop at a time. Watch what happens with one drop before dropping another. The salt will make fissures in the ice, which the paint fills, making spectacular channels.
6. Keep dripping and dropping and you could make a tunnel right through the ice.
7. Take photos of the stages and make a photo sequence on the computer.

Wild volcanoes

Two messy activities in one!

What you need:

- A cup measure
- Six cups flour
- Two cups salt
- Four tablespoons cooking oil
- Two cups of water.
- A small empty lemonade bottle with its lid
- A baking pan
- Two tablespoons bicarbonate of soda
- **Warm water in a squeezy bottle** (this makes it easier to add the water)
- Red food colouring
- Washing-up liquid
- A funnel
- Vinegar
- A thin stick for stirring

What to do:

Stage 1

1. Mix the flour, salt, cooking oil and water together in the bowl.

2. Help the children to knead the mixture with their hands until it is smooth and firm (add more water if you need to). You need to make a soft, squidgy dough.

3. Stand the empty bottle (with the lid on) in the middle of the baking pan.

4. Now work with the children to build a volcano shape round the bottle with the dough, keeping the neck of the bottle level with the top of the volcano.

5. Put the volcano somewhere warm to harden. This will take a couple of days, but if you can leave it longer – over a weekend would be even better.

Top tip ⭐

Salt and flour dough can be stored for a few days in an airtight container or ziplock bag for future play. If it dries out, add a small amount of water before playing again.

50 fantastic ideas for messy play

Stage 2

1. When it is dry, the children can paint the volcano. Mixing a bit of PVA in the paint will make it shiny.

2. When the paint is dry, take the top off the bottle and use the funnel to fill the bottle about three quarters full of warm water and add some red food colouring.

3. Add eight drops of detergent to the bottle.

4. Add four or five tablespoons of bicarbonate of soda. (Start with four and add more if the vinegar is slow to work).

5. Slowly pour some vinegar into the bottle, and see your volcano erupt.

6. You can make your volcano erupt again by adding another spoonful of bicarbonate of soda and stirring the bottle with the stick.

Taking it forward

- Mix glitter with the soda dough to make your volcano sparkle.

- Make several volcanoes, paint them different colours and set them all off together.

What's in it for the children?

This activity is good for following instructions. Mixing and handling the dough is a great tactile experience.

Health & Safety

Baking soda and vinegar is not harmful but does taste nasty. Vinegar is acid and will sting cuts, or sore and sensitive skin.

Look down!

Mirror, mirror on the floor!

What you need:

- **Unbreakable mirrors** (several)
- **Small bowls**
- **Paint**
- **Small brushes, cotton buds**
- **PVA glue**
- **A camera**

Top tip ⭐

This activity is best done outside, but indoor mirror work is also fascinating for children.

Taking it forward

- Take the mirrors with you when you go on visits and outings, and take some 'look down' photos of the places you visit. The ceiling of a museum, the sky at the farm park, perhaps even the underneath of an elephant or a knight in armour!

What's in it for the children?

This activity makes children concentrate on what they see.

➕ Health & Safety

This activity must be done with unbreakable mirrors, which you can buy in different shapes from online providers.

What to do:

1. Take all the things you need outside and put them on the grass or ground. Look in the mirrors together and talk about what you can see. You may be surprised at the children's responses to seeing things on the ground that they usually see above them.

2. Look up and down at the reflections and the real things above your heads.

3. Now let the children take the mirrors on a walk, putting them down and looking at what they can see.

4. Next show the children how you can paint what you see directly onto the mirror by lying or kneeling down near the mirror and following the lines of trees, flowers and other things they can see in the mirror. Some children will like to use a brush or cotton bud, but encourage them to experiment with their fingers, or little sticks, feathers, grass stalks or other 'tools' they find.

5. Once each child is satisfied with his/her painting, leave it flat for a little while to dry (if you leave it any longer it might turn into a drip painting).

6. When the painting is dry, let the child hold it up and photograph them with their painting, or take the photo from behind the child, so their face appears on the mirror behind the paint! Surprisingly, the painting will often look even better if you turn it upside down.

7. Import the photos onto a computer so the children can see their work immediately.

8. Let children wash their own paintings off the mirrors, so someone else can do a mirror painting.

Pumpkin pies

Foam and sand – yum!

What you need:

- Cans of cheap shaving foam
- A big plastic bowl
- Foil pie tins and dishes
- Food colouring (yellow, orange, brown and blue work well)
- Spices (cinnamon, nutmeg, mixed spice)
- Damp sand
- Spoons, blunt knives or spreaders

Top tip ⭐

Use non-allergenic foam so everyone can join in.

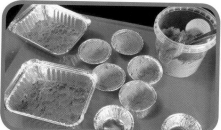

Taking it forward

- Make other flavours and perfumes of foam for cherry, apple or blackberry pies.

What's in it for the children?

Engaging additional senses adds to enjoyment and to learning. The sense of smell is the most powerful of our five senses.

➕ **Health & Safety**

Foam tastes horrible, so warn children that however good it smells, it's not for eating!

What to do:

1. Spray lots of foam into the bowl – the children love to do this by themselves.

2. Add food colouring – if you want it to look like pumpkin, start with lots of yellow, then add orange and a bit of brown or blue to darken it.

3. Mix the foam so that it is an even colour.

4. Make your pie filling smell like a real pie by adding a couple of teaspoons of spice. Cinnamon and nutmeg are traditional in American pumpkin pies.

5. When the pie filling looks and smells right, offer some foil pie tins, and some damp sand to make a pumpkin pie bases. Press sand into the bottom and sides of the pans - it will look just like biscuit crumb base.

6. Now use big spoons to ladle the gloopy foam into the pies, smoothing the tops with your hands or plastic spoons.

7. Set up a pie shop or café in your outdoor area, with a table and chairs.

Beautiful, bouncy beads

Magic swelling water beads

What you need:

- Packets of clear water beads
- Bowls or jugs
- Water colour paints, water based inks or food colouring

What to do:

To make coloured water beads

1. Put some dry water beads in each bowl.
2. Add water and a different colour to each.
3. Fill the bowls to the top with water and watch what happens.
4. Add more water as the beads soak it all up.
5. Add more colour if the beads seem pale when you fish a few out.
6. Tip the beads in a water tray or plastic box, or just on a tray (pour carefully, they are very bouncy!).

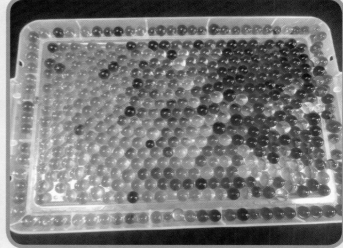

Health & Safety

Water beads are completely safe, but warn the children not to eat them, and wash your hands after playing with any of the glowing activities.

Top tip ⭐

Get water beads online, they are very cheap, and you get a lot for your money!

What to do:

To make glow-in-the-dark water beads

1. Break open the yellow highlighters (adult only) and put them in the bowl or jug.

2. Run or pour water over the pens to get all the yellow ink out. Cut open the fillings, squeeze the spongy insides and then discard the remaining pens.

3. Remove all the plastic pieces from the glow water.

4. Unpack the water beads and put them with the glowing water in a bowl, transparent jug or plastic box until the beads have swelled up to full size.

5. When the beads have stopped growing, take them somewhere dark and shine the black light on them to make them glow!

6. Tip the glowing beads in a tray for play in the dark.

What you need:

- Non-toxic yellow highlighters
- Scissors
- Water
- A jug or bowl to catch the 'glow water'
- Clear water beads
- A 'black light' lamp (available from the internet or an electrical supplier for about £5).

Taking it forward

■ Freeze your glowing water beads for a new experience. Put the beads in a plastic box, and put the box in the freezer overnight. On the following day, tip these into some water in a water tray or builder's tray. Discard these beads when they have melted.

■ Cook some thin rice noodles and soak them in glow water. Use these with plastic spiders for spider play in a creepy dark place.

What's in it for the children?

Helping to make things change is a very exciting operation, and playing with the sensory materials is a new experience.

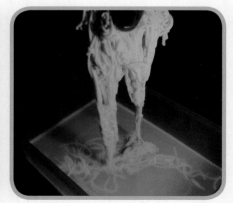

Paint it rough
Thick paint prints

What you need:

- Cup suitable for measuring
- Six to eight cups plain flour
- Aromatherapy oils, Kool-Aid or herbs and spices
- Dry sand
- Water
- Food colouring
- Bowls, spoons
- Scrapers, combs, plastic paint scrapers, or scrapers made from card with patterns cut in the edges
- A smooth table top and some thick paper

Top tip ⭐

Kool-Aid is an American drink powder. You can buy it online and use it to colour and perfume play materials. It is very sweet, so we do not recommend it for drinking!

Taking it forward

- Try room fragrance oils, baby oil, lavender oil or other spices for some different scent experiences.
- Spread foil on the table and try painting on that.

What's in it for the children?

This is a great sensory activity. Get the children to use words to describe the smells and how the paint feels.

Health & Safety

Make sure you know of any children who have allergic reactions.

What to do:

1. Put about six to eight cups of flour in a bowl.
2. Add water, slowly and a little at a time. You want the paint to be thick and textured, so don't add too much water.
3. Divide the mixture into several smaller bowls.
4. Add some perfume and colour to each bowl. This could be:

    a. drops of perfumed oil and some food colouring

    b. herbs or spices and yellow or orange paint

    c. a couple of teaspoons of Kool-Aid powder.
5. Add some dry sand to each bowl with a teaspoon, a little at a time, and stir until the paint is thick and grainy but still liquid enough to pour. Mix the paint well.
6. Put the paint bowls on a smooth tabletop.
7. Put spoons in the paint, so the children can scoop some onto the table, and put the scrapers and tools nearby.
8. Use the tools to make swirls, lines, circles, experimenting with shapes and patterns. Mix the colours.
9. Take a print by gently placing a piece of paper on top of your pattern. Smooth the paper with your palms, then gently pull it off to see your pattern.

A sweet solution

Glossy milk paint and spaghetti brushes

What you need:

- Ready-mixed paint
- Condensed milk
- Tablespoon
- Teaspoons
- Small bowls
- Paper
- Uncooked spaghetti and elastic bands
- A small amount of cooking oil in a bowl
- Hot water in a jug, or a pan of boiling water (adult only)

Top tip ⭐

Add some fluorescent paints and use a battery powered black light – you can get this online.

Taking it forward

- Make paint with cornflour, self raising flour, chocolate pudding, custard, instant coffee, baby rice, soap flakes, syrup, oatmeal, sugar, baby powder, baking powder or flour.

- Make some more unusual brushes by cutting lengths of raffia, folding them in half, and fixing each one with a pipe cleaner or elastic band, or offering, sticks, bunches of straws, hair 'scrunchies' etc.

What's in it for the children?

Any familiar activity is given new life by using something new – a new tool, or a new paint will inspire new work!

➕ Health & Safety

The paint looks and smells very sweet. Warn the children not to eat it!

What to do:

1. Prepare your spaghetti 'brushes' by winding elastic bands round small handfuls of dry spaghetti.

2. Put the ends of these 'brushes' in a jug or pan of very hot water until the ends have softened, but have not gone too soft.

3. Remove the brushes from the water and gently dip the softened ends in a little oil – this stops the spaghetti from sticking together.

4. Put two or three spoonfuls of paint in each bowl.

5. Add an equal amount of condensed milk.

6. Mix the condensed milk and paint very thoroughly. If it is too sticky, add a very small amount of water.

7. Unroll the paper, and tape it on the floor or over several tables, so more children can work simultaneously .

8. Put the paint and the painting tools out, talking with the children as you look at each one.

9. Now let the children experiment with the new painting tools, using the spaghetti brushes to swirl and make patterns with the paint.

10. You could also add some small paintbrushes or sponges to the experience.

11. If you have used fluorescent paint, shine your black light on the pictures to make the shiny paint light up.

paper birds
Papier mâché feathered friends

What you need:

- Lots of newspapers
- Plastic mixing bowl or bucket
- Wooden spoon
- Potato masher
- Wallpaper paste and warm water
- Ready-mixed paints
- PVA glue
- Straws, beads, googly eyes, feathers

Top tip ⭐

Papier mâché is gloriously messy, but preparation and drying take time. Have these stages running alongside other activities over several days, so the children don't lose interest.

Taking it forward

■ Produce different birds and make a display on a log or in some home-made nests. Share some bird stories (*Owl Babies* by Martin Waddell, *Rosie's Walk* by Pat Hutchins, *Make Way for Ducklings* by Robert McCloskey, *Farmer Duck* by Martin Wadell).

■ Play some birdcalls (try http://www. british-birdsongs.uk/ or BBC Tweet of the Day).

What's in it for the children?

This activity is excellent for practicing fine motor skills and maintaining interest over a long activity. If children work together on the birds it's good for learning to co-operate.

✚ Health & Safety

Buy non-fungicidal paste.

What to do:

1. Tear the newspaper into strips, and then tear the strips into squares. Children may tire of doing this, so prepare some earlier to have in reserve. Don't use scissors – torn edges are better.

2. Mix some wallpaper paste in a bowl or bucket, following the instructions on the packet. Use warm water, and mix until smooth – it should be as thick as yogurt, so add more wallpaper paste or water until you get the right consistency.

3. Put the newspaper squares into the paste and stir with a wooden spoon. Now let the children use the potato masher to squidge the paper down. As the mixture cools, the children can put their hands in and squeeze the mixture until it is a very thick paste without lumps. Add some more warm water, to keep the mixture sloppy.

4. When the papier mâché is well mixed, the children can make it into bird body shapes by squeezing it with their fingers, or forming the body round a ball.

5. Leave the birds somewhere warm to dry completely. Depending on the wetness of your mixture, and the place they are stored, this could take several days.

6. When the birds are dry, make some legs for them from wire or pipe cleaners, and paint the birds with paint mixed with PVA to make them shiny. Add a beak made from card or a drinking straw, some eyes and wings, tails or crests from feathers.

Blowing in the wind

Make a garden frieze just by blowing!

What you need:

- Long sheets of paper
- **Liquid watercolours in pastel colours** (blues, greens, purples, pinks)
- **Paint mixed with a bit of PVA glue in small containers – a range of strong flower colours** (yellow, red, blue, pink, purple)
- **Straws**
- **Plastic pipettes**
- **Thick paintbrushes**
- **Newspaper for blowing practice**

What to do:

1. Explain to the children what you are going to do.

2. Unroll a long sheet of paper on the floor or outside, holding it down with bricks or stones.

3. Mix paint until it is very runny and paint the background with big brushes.

4. While the background is drying show the children how to blow paint around on a piece of newspaper, carefully lifting and dropping small amounts of paint with a pipette and using a straw to blow the paint into the shape of a flower, leaf or stem.

5. Check that the paint is the right consistency, not too runny or it will lose shape, but not too thick or it will be hard to blow into shapes. Add more PVA if it is too runny, more water if it is too thick.

6. When the background is dry, use the straw blowing method to make a garden full of flowers and leaves.

7. Add butterflies, bees, and other insects to your garden scene, and display it in your room.

Taking it forward

- Talk with the children about using this method to make creepy night-time pictures. Make a night background with runny paint and big brushes, and then make straw blowing pictures of spiders and monsters on the background with black shiny paint. Add some googly eyes.

- Make an underwater scene, space picture or background for a story display.

What's in it for the children?

Controlling fingers, eyes and breathing is a great practice for other activities needing concentration.

Top tip ⭐

Snip a small hole in each straw near the top to stop children from sucking the paint in by mistake!

Snow gak

Make a sparkly snowman

What you need:

- **250ml white glue** (the clear version is best)
- **250ml warm water**
- **Two teaspoons borax and two cups of warm water**
- **Very small polystyrene balls, grains or seeds** (we used couscous)
- **Large bowls**
- **Small bowl**

To decorate the snowman:

- **Pipe cleaners**
- **Googly eyes**
- **Buttons**

Top tip ⭐

The texture of this gloopy mixture is the real fascination – it's also very stretchy!

Taking it forward

- Add colour to your gak and make some more shapes.
- Try making some of the other sensory mixtures in the book, and talk about how they feel different. Which is the most stretchy, the softest, the slimiest?

What's in it for the children?

This activity is excellent for practicing fine motor skills.

➕ Health & Safety

Borax is safe to use but not good to eat, and you should wash hands after use. If you want to avoid using borax, see the contents page for sensory activities using different ingredients.

What to do:

1. Empty the glue into a large bowl. Add the warm water. Mix until it is thoroughly combined.
2. Add the polystyrene balls, grains or seeds. Stir until they are incorporated into the mixture.
3. Dissolve two teaspoons of borax into two cups of very warm water in a large bowl (adult only.)
4. Pour the glue mixture into the bowl with the borax mixture. Almost immediately, snow gak will be formed.
5. Stir it until it comes together. You will have some liquid left in the bowl, which you can just pour away.
6. Now the snow gak is ready to be played with! It's really stretchy and pliable. See who can make the longest gak rope!
7. Since this is snow gak, the children can make snowmen. Stretch the snow gak into snowman shapes on a tabletop. Decorate the snowmen with buttons and pipe cleaners.
8. Photograph the snowmen and use the photos for Christmas cards.
9. The gak will stay stretchy, so other children can use it afterwards.

Rollerball
Blowing games with paint

What you need:

- Table tennis balls or golf balls
- Cat litter trays or other deep sided containers such as a baking pans
- Paint
- Foil containers
- Straws

Top tip ⭐

Ask your local golf club for old golf balls.

What to do:

1. This activity is good for co-operation, arrange for two or three children to work together. Once it has been set up, the children could manage it independently.

2. Line the bottom of the pans with paper.

3. Pour some paint into the foil dishes.

4. Now the children can dip the balls into the paint and manipulate the tins to make the balls move in patterns.

5. Show them how to use a straw to blow a painty table tennis ball around to make the pattern.

6. Spoon a bit more paint straight onto the paper and blow the balls through the paint.

7. Try a race from one end of the tray to the other, with two children blowing a ball each.

8. Remove the paper and replace it for another go.

Taking it forward

- Capture some of your painted balls in a shoebox. Line the box with paper, pop the balls inside, tape the top on and give the box a really good shake. Peep inside to check if you have a good pattern, and add more paint if you like.

- Inflate a paddling pool, or offer a turkey roasting pan for the same game, showing the children how to work together to manage rocking the container to make the balls move.

What's in it for the children?

Learning to work together is a skill some children find difficult and need plenty of practice to perfect.

➕ Health & Safety

Ensure that the soil is not contaminated with any animal faeces and that the children wash their hands thoroughly afterwards.

Rice is nice
Colourful rice play

What you need:

- A large quantity of uncooked white rice
- Food colouring
- One tablespoon of white vinegar for every cup of dry rice – vinegar sterilises the rice, so it is safe to use for longer
- Ziplock bags
- Baking trays or plastic plates

Top tip ⭐

Big quantities are the secret to this activity - buy bargain bags of rice from supermarkets.

What to do:

1. Decide how many different colours you want, and put a tablespoon of vinegar in a ziplock bag for each colour.

2. Add a different food colouring to each bag or mix two colours to make new ones.

3. Add a cup or two of uncooked rice to each bag.

4. Do up the zips and get the children to help you to massage the rice until it is all coloured.

5. Tip each bag onto a different baking tray or plate. Spread the rice out in a thin layer.

6. Put the plates/trays in a warm place (on a radiator or in a sunny window). Stir the rice from time to time to speed up drying.

7. When your rice is dry, you can use it for free play and for art and craft projects.

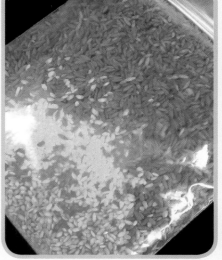

✚ Health & Safety

Be aware that small objects can find their way into ears and nostrils – be vigilant.

Taking it forward : A little project

Coloured rice is a useful alternative to sand and water for mathematical explorations.

1. You need a plastic milk container with a handle, and a clear plastic drinks bottle

2. Make a scoop from the milk bottle with a handle, by cutting it as shown in the picture here. You can also use this scoop as a funnel by removing the lid.

3. Make a funnel by cutting the top off the plastic drink bottle as shown.

4. Make a measuring cup by using the bottom of the bottle. Check the capacity of this cup by filling a kitchen cup measure with coloured rice, pouring this into your home-made one, and marking the level with a permanent marker.

5. Now use your mathematics equipment to explore the coloured rice and other resources. Older children can use these objects to start exploring estimation, capacity, measuring and comparing.

What's in it for the children?

Early mathematics and science needs lots of free play with materials and equipment before moving on to more formal experiments.

Sponge fun

Make your own big foam

What you need:

- A water or sand tray
- A piece of furnishing foam to fit exactly in your water tray
- Washing-up liquid or liquid soap
- Food colouring
- Implements of all sorts – small pans, foil dishes, moulds, cups, spoons, small sponges, sponge balls, bowls, plastic bottles, old credit or loyalty cards, small world characters, cars etc.

Top tip ⭐

It is worth going to a foam shop, as you might get a free offcut!

Taking it forward

- Mix some food colouring with a jug of water and add this to the sponge. What happens?
- If the children press their hands onto the foam, the impression will stay for a few moments. Talk about this and try other things to make impressions.

What's in it for the children?

This activity is open-ended, and will encourage children's imagination and language.

✚ Health & Safety

To avoid stagnant water collecting in the bottom of the tray, prop the foam up on its end every night so the water drains out.

What to do:

1. Start every day with a clean, almost dry sponge.
2. Add a small amount of water and a couple of squirts of washing-up liquid or liquid soap.
3. The first time you use the sponge, don't offer any utensils or other resources, just let the children squeeze and squish the foam, punching it and poking it till the surface is covered with foam.
4. The bubbles from the foam will be very small and, different from any other bubble activity, so exploring these and using them to fill things will fascinate some children. You can offer a box of small resources – yogurt pots cups, spoons for scooping and filling.
5. Offer other collections of items, such as toy cars, plastic tools, plates, plastic coffee cups, jugs, funnels, so the children can explore the unique nature of this foam. However, the major attraction of the activity will probably be just making more bubbles! As children play, use language such as smaller, bigger, pour, fill, drip, slow; and squeeze, squash, squish, press to expand their descriptive vocabularies.

The big art brush off

A new use for an old toothbrush

What you need:

- **Old electric toothbrush - rotary and oscillating heads will give different results** (don't worry, the brush handle will not be damaged in the process)
- **Paint – ideally this should be the consistency of cream** (if it is thicker it won't spread, if it is thinner it will blob and run)
- **Paper**
- **Water** (to clean the brushes)

Top tip ⭐

If you haven't got an outdoor tap, buy a big water container with a tap from a camping shop.

Taking it forward

- Check out http://www.techdigest. tv/2014/11/watch-a-winter-mural-created-with-just-an-electric-toothbrush.html. This artist made a huge picture with his electric toothbrush by brushing the moss off a wall. See if you can find some mossy stones, paving or even a wall to make a picture of your own.

- Paint part of your path or patio with ready-mixed paint and then use the electric toothbrush to make a pattern or picture by brushing off the paint.

What's in it for the children?

This is a good activity for getting children to predict 'What will happen if…?'. Don't miss the opportunity to talk with the children about the proper use of a toothbrush.

What to do:

1. It is best to do this activity outdoors as it can be very messy!

2. Spread out the paper on the floor and hold it down with big bricks.

3. Dip the toothbrush head in the paint and lay the toothbrush on the paper you have spread out.

4. Turn the toothbrush on and watch it spin. It should go about in circles. Nudge it if it needs a bit of encouragement, or if it gets too close to the edge of the paper.

5. Rinse the brush and apply a new colour. Try it again. The more colours you use, the more interesting the brush art will look.

6. Try adding to your picture by holding the brush by the handle and using the spinning end to paint.

Rainbow fingers
Fingers through foam

What you need:

- Several kitchen trays in different sizes
- Kitchen foil
- Masking tape
- Ready-mixed paint
- PVA glue
- Paintbrushes
- Cans of cheap shaving foam

What to do:

1. Cover the trays with foil, making sure that the foil goes up and over the sides.
2. Mix paints with a good squeeze of PVA in each colour. Pour into small bowls or pots.
3. Work with the children to completely cover the bottom of the trays with paint, in stripes, spots, wavy lines and zigzags. Don't leave any gaps, and avoid pools of paint, which will take too long to dry.
4. Leave to dry, preferably overnight.
5. Let the children squirt shaving foam all over the painted pattern and smooth it out with their hands, so the painting is completely covered.
6. Use fingers, paintbrushes or cotton buds to draw in the foam and reveal the magical colours underneath.
7. Smooth the foam over to hide the colours and begin another picture.

Top tip ⭐

If you do the first part of this activity at the end of the day, it will be dry for stage two the following morning.

Taking it forward

- Put a small amount of paint in a ziplock bag and fasten the zip (you may want to secure it with tape as well). Flatten the bag and let the children smooth the paint out all over the inside of the bag using flat hands. Then using one finger, draw a picture or pattern that shows what is underneath the bag. Put the bag on top of wrapping paper or magazine pictures, and the children can move the paint round to show different parts of the picture underneath.
- Make some bigger versions in a builder's tray or even on a smooth tabletop.

What's in it for the children?

Isolating index fingers in this activity is really good practice for writing.

✚ Health & Safety

Foam is slippery on the floor, so be careful of spills.

Little squirts
Squirty balloons

What you need:

- **Large sheets of paper**
- **Balloons**
- **Water paint in several colours** (thinly mixed)
- **A turkey baster or a small funnel**
- **Cloth tape** (often sold as 'gaffer' or 'duct' tape)
- **A needle** (adult only)

Top tip ⭐

This can be messy, so do it where spills don't matter and it's easy to clean up.

Taking it forward

- Try doing this activity with some cheap rubber gloves – fill these with paint and squirt through one or more fingers.
- Try making multiple holes in a balloon. See what shapes you can make.

What's in it for the children?

This is a good creative activity. Squirting the balloons gives excellent practice in hand control.

✚ Health & Safety

Balloons can be a choking hazard. Don't let children put them in their mouths or try to blow them up.

What to do:

1. Pin up the sheets of paper in a suitable spot.
2. Using the baster, squirt a generous amount (several tablespoons) of paint into each balloon.
3. Add some water (with the baster) and tie the ends of the balloons.
4. Stick a small piece of cloth tape to each balloon.
5. Carefully push the pin through the tape to make a small hole in each balloon (an adult should help younger children with this).
6. Aim streams of paint at the paper by squeezing the balloons. Don't stand too close, but not so far away the stream of paint doesn't reach.
7. Make shapes, mix colours. Let the children have a colour each, then swap.
8. Put your balloon in a small bowl and watch the paint fountain!

Edibubbles

Feel about in pasta and pearls

What you need:

- Tapioca pearls
- Spaghetti
- A large saucepan
- Water
- Cooking oil
- Colander or big sieve
- Small plastic bowls, foil dishes
- Food colouring
- A builder's tray, water tray or big plastic box

Top tip ⭐

Look for 'quick cook' tapioca pearls in Asian grocery shops – these cook in five minutes.

What to do:

1. Boil plenty of water and cook the tapioca pearls according to the instructions on the box or packet. Once cooked, drain the pearls and run them under cold water until they are cold. (Adult only.)

2. To make coloured pearls, divide the cooked pearls into several bowls, add a few drops of food colouring to each bowl and stir until they are evenly coloured.

3. Leave to soak for five minutes, then tip into a sieve and rinse under cold water. The pearls will be vibrant colours but the colour won't come off on children's hands.

4. Cook the spaghetti in water, with a few drops of food colouring, according to the instructions on the packet. Separate batches of red, blue, green and purple work well. Drain each batch and place into a bowl or other container. Add a tablespoon of oil to each bowl while the pasta is still warm. You now have slimy spaghetti.

5. Tip the spaghetti and the tapioca pearls into a big container and leave it for the children to explore with their hands!

6. You can store the pearls in a plastic box of water – they will keep for several days.

Taking it forward

- Use mixed dried food items such as couscous, rice, pasta shapes for a different feel and look. Ask parents to bring in out of date packets from their store cupboards.

- Try mixing several different sorts of wet items – beads, cooked pastas, tapioca pearls, coloured water beads, noodles, rice or couscous. These mixtures should be discarded at the end of the day.

What's in it for the children?

A wide number of different sensory experiences are essential for a rounded development. Different substances will engage different children.

Let's face it
A new look for dolls

What you need:

- Cornflour
- Skin moisturiser or baby lotion
- Whole milk
- Water
- Food colouring
- Small bowls
- Teaspoons for stirring
- Small paintbrushes
- Cotton buds
- Tissues and baby wipes
- Dolls

Taking it forward

- Once they have had some practice on the dolls, the children may want to paint each other's faces. Supervise this carefully.

- Try painting some animal faces. They'll need pictures to copy from.

What's in it for the children?

Any sort of painting is good for fine motor development. Producing a well-executed design requires precision and control.

Health & Safety

The paint is harmless, but warn children to keep it away from their eyes.

What to do:

1. For each colour, mix one teaspoon cornflour, half a teaspoon of whole milk and a quarter teaspoon of water until well blended. Add a little moisturiser to each bowl and mix again

2. Add a different food colouring to each bowl, a drop at a time.

3. Once you think it is dark enough, add a drop or two more as it will lighten up when it dries (try a bit on your hand if you're not sure).

4. Put all the dolls in their buggies or chairs.

5. The children can now use the paintbrushes and cotton buds to paint the dolls' faces (and hands, arms and legs).

6. Their first attempts may be a mess, but encourage them to keep going. The paint is easily removed with a damp tissue or baby wipe, so they can start again.

7. Take some photos of the painted dolls.

Top tip ★

Add some glitter to some of the paints to make the doll faces sparkle.

Chalk face

Wash the faces off the wall

What you need:

- **Water balloons and filler** (a filler is usually included with a packet of balloons)
- **A large plastic drinks bottle** (preferably 2l)
- **Playground chalks**

Top tip ⭐

Don't overfill the balloons. A 2 l bottle should fill about ten balloons.

Taking it forward

- Draw a big circle on the playground or patio and draw smaller circles inside each circle – number them. The children stand outside the circle and lob the balloons, aiming for the numbers.

- Drop filled balloons into a bowl of water to see how long it takes to overflow.

What's in it for the children?

Any aiming and throwing practice improves hand/eye coordination for writing and reading.

✚ Health & Safety

Water balloons can be a choking hazard. Don't let children put them in their mouths or try to blow them up by blowing into them.

What to do:

1. Fill the bottle with water and screw on the balloon filler.

2. Stand the bottle upright and fit a water balloon over the end of the filler. Don't squeeze yet. Invert the bottle and squeeze so that water goes into the balloon. When the balloon is about the size of a tennis ball twist the neck, take it off the filler and tie it. Repeat until there are enough balloons for each child to have several.

3. Get the children to use the chalk to draw faces on a wall, the side of a shed or a smooth fence. Make the faces different sizes.

4. Children can throw the balloons at the faces they've drawn to wash the chalk off. Make it a game – they score a point if they hit a face. They'll need to throw the balloons hard to make them burst. Retrieve any balloons that don't burst, and throw them again.

5. Gradually the water will wash off the faces, leaving the wall or fence clean.

6. When you've finished, protect the environment by picking up all the bits of broken balloon.

The twang's the thang
Elastic band art

What you need:

- A baking tray – one for each pair of children
- Some large, stretchy rubber bands for each tray
- Ready-mixed paint – four different colours for each tray (it needs to be thick, so add some flour or PVA)
- Paintbrush for each colour
- A4 paper

Taking it forward

- Add some more bands, either on the long sides or the short sides and try that.
- Do some fly swatter painting. Drop some blobs of paint on a large sheet of paper and swat them. The paint will fly, so you might want to use safety goggles for this extension.

What's in it for the children?

With this one the process is more important than the product. Experimenting is important, and these activities offer good opportunities for teamwork.

✚ Health & Safety

Take care with the rubber bands. Ones that ping can also sting.

What to do:

1. Make sure the paint is near the trays to avoid dripping.
2. Put a sheet of paper in the bottom of each baking tray.
3. Help the children to stretch between four and six rubber bands at equal distances around the long sides of the tray (see photo).
4. Paint each of the rubber bands a different colour. Use plenty of paint, but apply it carefully so it doesn't drip on to the paper too much.
5. Pull each rubber band back and let go. It's best to work in pairs – one person can paint and one can twang the bands as soon as they are painted, so the paint doesn't have chance to dry.
6. Let the children keep twanging the bands until they are happy with their pattern.
7. Remove the paper and replace with a new piece.

Top tip ⭐
This can be really messy! Be prepared.

Splatter rolls!

Different decorating rollers

What you need:

- Cheap decorating rollers
- Large, thick elastic bands
- Ready-mixed paint
- Decorator's paint trays, baking trays or plastic boxes
- Masking tape
- Roll of paper (lining paper is cheaper than display rolls)

Top tip ⭐

Try using a cheap roller with an extending handle, so it can be used standing up.

What to do:

1. You can use the rollers with their sponge or fluffy covers on or off. Some have a useful metal frame that can be covered with elastic bands.
2. Loop or tie several elastic bands round the wires (see photos).
3. Pour some paint in trays. You may want to add a little water, to make the paint thinner.
4. Make sure the children are well protected from splashes.
5. Spread some paper on the floor, and tape it down with masking tape.
6. Roll the roller gently in the paint, so the elastic bands get really painty.
7. Now roll the roller on the paper to make splashy, springy patterns.
8. Try the activity again with another colour.

Taking it forward

- Tie other things on your rollers – strips of fabric, lengths of string or wool or strips of plastic from carrier bags.
- Stick paper on an outside wall. Now try elastic band painting on a vertical surface.

What's in it for the children?

Many families deter their children from messy play! This activity really releases children from their inhibitions.

✚ Health & Safety

Be careful that elastic bands don't spring back and hurt someone.

Pour tall
Spectacular paint towers

What you need:

- **Squares of stiff card** (from a strong cardboard box)
- **Small blocks of wood or small boxes** (see photos)
- **Trays or space to catch drips** (we used a plastic box top)
- **A glue gun** (adult only)
- **Lots of paint in lots of different colours**
- **Plenty of PVA glue**
- **Disposable plastic or paper cups**
- **Paintbrushes or spoons to stir the paint**
- **A camera**

Top tip ⭐

Buy big cans of PVA from the builders' section of DIY stores, it's much cheaper.

For individual towers

Before you do this activity, watch the following YouTube video with the children – it shows an artist making these towers: https://www.youtube.com/watch?v=d6egUsZvWu4

What to do:

1. Glue the wooden pieces or small boxes in the middle of the square cards, using the glue gun (adult only). Let the children watch as you prepare the activity.

2. Put the towers somewhere flat and firm. This is best done indoors unless you can guarantee a windless day!

3. Put paint in plenty of small plastic pots or waxed cups (those used in fast food restaurants for ketchup work well). About four to five cups of paint will do to start. Add at least an equal amount of PVA glue. The more glue, the shinier the finished tower will be.

4. If the children have seen the video they will know what to do next - they must pour the paint over the tower! Your role is just to make sure they have plenty of paint, and to remind the children that they should pour slowly and gently onto the middle of the top of the tower.

5. When each child has poured as much paint as they want over their tower, leave it for as long as possible before moving it to a safe place where the children can admire it with their friends. The paint will probably continue moving for some time.

What you need:

- Several strong cartons in varying sizes
- A builder's tray
- A large piece of wood, wider than the biggest box you are using, but small enough to fit inside the builder's tray.
- White emulsion paint and brushes
- Lots of paint (mixed with PVA) in plastic cups
- A glue gun
- A camera

For the group tower
What to do:

This activity is for a group of children, working together, although they don't all need to be involved all the time.

1. Use the glue gun (adult only) to close the boxes shut as smoothly as possible. This is important to the final design, as the flow of paint should be smooth and even down each side.

2. Glue the boxes to the middle of the board, with plenty of glue, so the tower is level and firm.

3. Paint the boxes with emulsion paint to cover the printing on the sides.

4. Put the structure somewhere level and spacious (perhaps on the floor).

5. Put the paint on a table nearby.

6. Prepare plenty of paint and PVA mixture in lots of colours and shades, in plastic cups. Make sure the cups are not more than half full.

7. Start to work with the children by gently pouring a cup of paint over the middle of the top box, slowly emptying the whole cup. As long as the structure is level, the paint should pour over all four edges and down the sides of the box. Watch what happens.

8. Now slowly pour another colour onto the top of the box, on top of the first.

9. Take turns to pour more colours on slowly until you agree that you have finished – or you run out of paint. The paint should flow down the sides of the box, making patterns on the box and pooling in patterns at the bottom.

10. Take plenty of photos!

11. Leave your creation to dry, then gently lift it out of the builder's tray and display it in your setting.

What's in it for the children?

This is a most enjoyable activity, particularly for a group. Practice in control and concentration is very beneficial for children.

Car wash
Small world car maintenance

What you need:

- Paint
- Thin paintbrushes
- Shaving foam
- Warm water and washing-up liquid
- Toy cars, planes, trucks etc
- A builder's tray or big plastic box lid (this will be the paint shop)
- A tray or second plastic lid (this will be the car wash)
- An empty water tray or big plastic box (this will be the rinsing station)
- Blue food colouring
- Small sponges
- Road mat if available

What to do:

1. Mix some paint in small containers. Adding a drop of PVA glue will make the paint stick better.
2. Set out the paint shop (the shallow tray) with paints and brushes nearby. Line up the cars ready for the game.
3. Fill the car wash stage with shaving foam.
4. Fill the rinsing station with warm water and a few drops of blue food colouring.
5. Now suggest that the children could paint the cars in new colours at the paint shop, and then try them out on the road map.
6. When they have played with their newly painted cars for a bit, they can wash the paint off in the car wash and rinse them in the rinsing station.
7. This process can then be repeated using other colours.
8. When the game is over, wash away the paint and soap with a hose or bucket of water. Children will love to help with the sweeping up.

> **Top tip** ⭐
>
> Buy cheap toy cars from your local bargain shop or supermarket.

Taking it forward

- You could repaint different small world collections – dinosaurs, farm animals, superheroes etc.

What's in it for the children?

Using small brushes is a good way to improve fine motor skills in an enjoyable activity.

✚ Health & Safety

Hose the soapy water away to prevent slipping.

Sweep it

A messy work out with mops and brooms

What you need:

- Child-sized, or small, light adult mops and brooms
- Buckets and big bowls
- Powder paint or ready-mixed paint
- Washing-up liquid
- A big outdoor space

What to do:

1. Mix some washing-up liquid with water in the buckets.
2. Scatter some powder paint on the ground outside.
3. Give the children the mops and brooms, and stand back.
4. Let the children work freely mopping, cleaning the paint, and making wet marks on the ground.
5. At the end of the session, the children could wash any remaining paint away with a hose.

Top tip ⭐

Buy child-sized tools online, and buy the best quality you can afford. They will last much longer.

Taking it forward

- On a wet day, put some powder paint in paper bags (plastic bags will not work for this activity) and screw the ends of the bags up. Drop these paint bombs on the ground outside and watch what happens. Use bubbly water to clear up.

- Let the children have access to small quantities of washing-up liquid or bubble solution and water to paint and mop outside. They will do little harm as long as they just use water. A window cleaner's kit of squeegees and cloths will make the play even more realistic.

What's in it for the children?

This activity exercises muscles in the core of the body, as well as shoulders, arms, hands and fingers that are needed to prepare fine motor skills.

✚ Health & Safety

If you use adult-sized brooms and mops, you could cut the handles down a bit to avoid accidents.

Salty seascapes
Paint with salt

What you need:

- PVA glue in small squeezy bottles
- Sheets of card – use cut cereal packets or cartons
- 2kg salt
- Plastic spoons
- A plastic box big enough for the card pieces
- Water based blue paint, mixed fairly thin
- Small paintbrushes
- A jar of clean water
- Hair spray to fix

What to do:

1. Pour the salt into a flat container, such as a clean cat litter tray.
2. Put the paint and brushes near the activity.
3. Squeeze the glue onto a piece of card to make a wave pattern or a picture of the sea. Use plenty of glue.
4. Lift the card very carefully and put it in the tray of salt.
5. Use a plastic spoon to scoop salt onto the card so your pattern or picture is completely covered.
6. Count to ten.
7. Now carefully tip the card so the spare salt tips back into the box.
8. Put the card flat on the table and dip a brush in the blue paint.
9. Touch the salt very gently with the brush. Don't paint or rub, just touch, and the paint will follow the lines of salt.
10. When the creation is finished, put it in a warm place to dry.
11. These paintings are fragile. When they are dry, protect them with hair spray.

Top tip ⭐

Get a few cat litter trays to use in art and craft activities.

Taking it forward

- Make bleach pictures. Paint a sheet of paper all over with diluted food colouring. Let it dry, then paint with a cotton bud dipped into a teaspoon of bleach. The bleach will make white lines in the coloured paint.

What's in it for the children?

Making their own changes to familiar ingredients is a magical thing for children, which can lead to a real interest in science.

✚ Health & Safety

Be careful if you use bleach in the follow-up activity.

Take your vitamins
A new glowing ingredient for sensory play

What you need:

- Cornflour
- Cup measure
- Vitamin B-20 complex tablets
- Warm water
- Rolling pin
- Ziplock bag
- Black light
- A small plastic storage basket with a handle (see photos)

What to do:

1. Put two to four tablets of Vitamin B into a ziplock bag and pound them into a powder with a rolling pin or brick (some versions of this vitamin glow more brightly than others – you may need to experiment).

2. Add the crushed tablets to two cups of warm water, and stir until completely dissolved.

3. Put two cups of cornflour in a bowl and add the vitamin water – the mixture should be runny and should drip from your fingers, if the mixture is too thick add a bit more water, if it is too runny add a bit more cornflour.

4. Pour into a water tray or a big plastic box, and explore with hands or with water toys and equipment. This mixture will work well without being in the dark.

5. You could take your glowing ooblek (this is what it is called in the USA) into a dark place and shine the black light on it as you lift it up to make strings from your fingers.

6. Put the ooblek in the basket and hang it up indoors or outside, so it pours out through the holes in long strands (see photos).

Top tip ⭐

This is a version of cornflour 'ooblek' with a 'glow in the dark' feature, but it does not use chemicals. You can get the vitamin tablets from a health food shop or online.

Taking it forward

- You can also use the tablets in a water tray to make glowing water. If you put your water tray somewhere dark or behind a curtain it brings a new world to the whole activity, especially during the winter months.

- Freeze the glowing water to make glowing ice cubes.

What's in it for the children?

Glowing stuff is magical to all children, and glowing ooblek will inspire them to engage and talk about what they are doing.

➕ Health & Safety

There is no danger to children even if they swallow small quantities of the vitamin. There is also no danger of it being taken in through the skin.

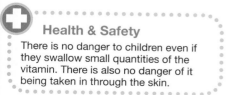

Snake sock bubbles

Novel bubble blowers

What you need:

For the blowers:

- Small plastic water bottles
- Children's socks
- Scissors
- Duct tape
- Thick elastic bands (big enough to go round a bottle)
- Food colouring

You also need:

- A big bottle of bubble mixture

Or some of the best bubble mixture, made by mixing in a bucket:

- 12 cups of water
- One cup of washing-up liquid
- One cup of cornflour
- Two tablespoons of baking powder (not baking soda!)

Some people add a little sugar to the mixture. Experiment to see if this works better with the brand of washing-up liquid you're using.

What to do:

If you are making your own bubble solution:

1. Put 12 cups of water in the bucket or bowl.
2. Slowly add the washing-up liquid. Be careful not to go too quickly or you may spoil your mixture.
3. Sprinkle over the baking powder and stir it in gently. Be careful not to make bubbles in the water as you stir.
4. Leave for at least an hour, preferably overnight before using.

Now make some snake bubble blowers:

5. Help the children to carefully cut the bottoms off the water bottles.
6. Push each bottle into a sock, cut end first, until the sock is tight over the end.
7. Fix the top of the sock to the bottle with an elastic band to make sure the sock is tight over the bottom of the bottle.
8. Secure it with an elastic band, and trim the extra sock off (you may need to help here).
9. Fasten tape round the top of the sock to make a secure fit round the bottle.
10. Put some of the bubble mixture in a shallow container or plastic box, take the tops off the bottles and dip the sock end in the mixture.
11. Now the children can blow down the bottles to make bubble snakes.
12. When the children have made their snakes, try dropping a little food colouring onto the socks and dipping again to make coloured snakes.

Top tip ⭐

If the bottles are too big, children may find it difficult to blow hard enough to make it work. So with taller bottles, make the cut about halfway up.

Taking it forward

Make some more bubble blowers from:

- Pipe cleaners: make shapes from pipe cleaners, making sure you have a handle. Try circles, stars or triangles.

- Drinking straws: choose small straws, as these will make fast flowing bubbles. Bunch some together and see how many you can get, then dip and try!

What's in it for the children?

Early science experiments enable children to explore the world in an enjoyable way; observation is the first step in scientific exploration.

✚ Health & Safety

Bubble mixture can make surfaces slippery. Warn the children, and avoid surfaces that could become slippery.

Party bucket

Anything goes with a painting party

What you need:

- Raffia and pipe cleaners
- Spaghetti
- Elastic bands
- Kitchen utensils and cleaning tools such as scourers, bath 'scrunchies', dishwashing brushes etc
- Chains of different sizes
- **Strong paper** (a roll of lining paper would be ideal)
- Small bowls for paint
- Ready-mixed paint

Top tip ⭐

Try bargain shops for cheap kitchen items.

Taking it forward

- You can paint with almost anything – how about hand sprays on a fence, fly swatters, skipping rope, vegetable or fruit nets filled with newspaper, sponges, water pistols.

- You can even print with a whole fish! This is called 'gyotaku' (pronounced ghio-ta-koo). You can do this by getting a medium to large whole fish, washed and dried. Paint your fish on one side, and press a sheet of paper gently on the fish. Lift it off and you will find a fish print on the paper!

What's in it for the children?

Any familiar activity is given new life by using something new – a new tool, or even a new paint texture will inspire new work!

What to do:

1. Before you start, collect some kitchen utensils such as fish slices, whisks, bottle brushes.

2. Buy some cheap cleaning items such as scourers, dish brushes, bath scrunchies.

3. Find or buy some short lengths of chain and rope of different thicknesses. Collect bottle tops, corks, toothbrushes, bunches of elastic bands, cotton wool balls – be imaginative!

4. Mix several colours of paint. Put each colour in a separate shallow bowl.

5. Unroll the paper, and hold it down with tape, big stones or bricks on a flat area outside. If you tape the paper on the floor or over several tables, more children can work at once.

6. Put the paint, the painting tools and the chains out, talking with the children as you look at each one, discussing how they could use them and how to work safely.

7. Now let the children experiment with the painting tools, dipping them in the bowls of paint and using them to make patterns on the paper.

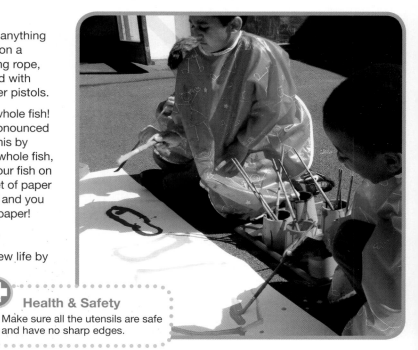

➕ Health & Safety

Make sure all the utensils are safe and have no sharp edges.

Polka dot slime

Stretchy spots and dots

An alternative to borax, this slime uses laundry detergent

What you need:

- A big bowl
- Wooden spoon
- A teaspoon
- PVA glue
- A cup measure
- Laundry detergent (preferably gel)
- A pack of fuzzy craft balls
- Food colouring (optional)

What to do:

1. Put about a cup of PVA glue into the bowl.
2. Add colouring if you wish.
3. Add laundry detergent a teaspoonful at a time, and stir thoroughly between each spoonful.
4. Keep stirring until the slime sticks together and leaves the side of the bowl. Keep it stringy! If your slime is at all sticky, add a tiny bit more laundry gel and knead it in until your slime is firm enough to play with.
5. Tip in the fuzzy balls and work these into the slime.
6. Now stretch and pull the slime so the bobbles move around inside it.

Top tip ⭐

Cheaper laundry gels work best for this activity.

Taking it forward

- Each time you make this slime, add something different – water beads, couscous, uncooked rice, orzo pasta, cooked spaghetti, flower petals, or spices and herbs all work well.

- Make perfumed slime with aromatherapy oils.

What's in it for the children?

This slime has a unique texture – use the play to extend children's vocabulary of descriptive words.

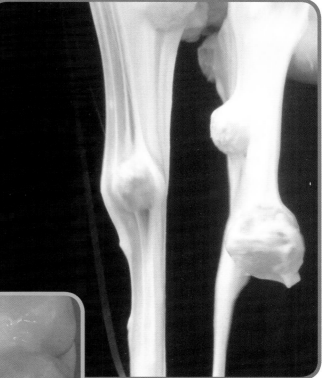

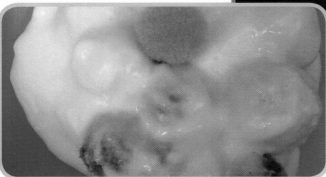

Health & Safety

Be aware of allergies among the children.

Funny feet!

Bubbly boots and spongy slippers

What you need:

- Bubble wrap
- Cheap foam sponges
- Ready-mixed paint in shallow trays
- Masking tape
- Elastic bands, Velcro straps, or wide elastic
- Scissors
- Paintbrushes
- A roll of paper
- Bricks or stones to hold the paper down
- Warm soapy water and towels

Top tip ⭐

Make sure your school or setting office knows how much you like to keep spare packaging!

Taking it forward

- Make bubble rollers from cardboard tubes covered in bubble wrap. Cut the bubble wrap narrower than the length of the tube to leave room for your hands. Cover with paint and roll on paper as if you were rolling pastry.

- Make bubble wrap prints. Paint on the bubbly side of the bubble wrap, put a piece of paper on top of the painted bubble wrap, smooth it gently, then lift the paper slowly off to reveal your print.

What's in it for the children?

Sensory experiences are very important for young learners, and this activity helps with sensation and with balance.

What to do:

1. Spread the paper roll on the floor indoors or outside, to make a big printing space.

2. Put two or three different colours of paint in shallow pans or dishes.

3. Explain what you are going to do, and ask for a volunteer. Let this child choose whether to stamp with bubble wrap or sponges on their feet.

For bubble wrap boots:

4. Cut two lengths of bubble wrap, long enough to cover the child's bare feet.

5. Roll up trousers, and wrap the child's feet in the bubble wrap, with the bubbles on the outside. Use tape to fix it securely on one foot or both.

6. Paint the bottoms of the bubble wrap boots with their choice of colour, or dip the 'boots' in a shallow dish of paint. Help the child to stand so they can walk, jump and even hop on the paper.

7. Repaint the boots when necessary.

For sponge feet:

8. Fix the sponges to the child's bare feet with elastic bands, Velcro™ or other fixing.

9. Let them dip their feet in the paint dishes and stamp or jump on the paper.

10. When the paper gets full of prints, replace it and start a new picture.

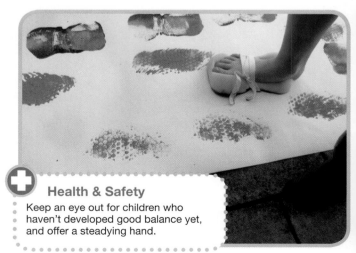

➕ Health & Safety

Keep an eye out for children who haven't developed good balance yet, and offer a steadying hand.

Splashbox

Take aim and just throw

What you need:

- **A large box** – the bigger the better
- **Box knife**
- **Lining paper**
- **Tape** (masking tape works well)
- **Paint trays**
- **Paint and water**
- **Tennis balls**
- **Sponges**

Top tip ⭐

Ask parents/carers to bring it any spare large packaging materials.

What to do:

1. Gather everything together. With the box knife cut one side out of the box (adult only).
2. Tape the lining paper to all five inside walls of the box.
3. Mix the paint, three parts paint to one part water.
4. Dip a tennis ball or sponge into one of the paint colours. Make sure it's soaked.
5. Throw the ball into the box from a few paces away.
6. Soak another ball in a different colour and throw that.
7. Keep throwing and bouncing the painty balls and sponges into the box.
8. When you have finished your bouncy painting, replace the paper and try with fluorescent paint.
9. When you have done with throwing the fluorescent balls, replace the missing side of the box, and shine a torch through a hole into the top of the box to make the paint glow.

Taking it forward

- Tape a very big box completely closed and cut a child-sized door in one side. Leave one side of the door for a hinge. Let the children decorate the inside of their secret box with paints, pens etc.

- Get some smaller boxes and do the same activity with small sponge balls.

What's in it for the children?

Any throwing activity improves hand/eye coordination, and will result in better hand control and fine motor skills.

Eat a monster

Easy edible bread fun

What you need:

(enough for four to six children):

- Cup and spoon measures
- Four cups strong white bread flour
- One sachet or one and a half teaspoons fast action dried yeast
- One and a half cups warm water
- One tablespoon olive oil
- Pastry brush
- Milk in a small cup
- Currants
- A large bowl
- Spoons
- Clean pastry boards
- Blunt knives, garlic press
- Baking trays
- Kitchen timer
- Clean tea towels

What to do:

1. Work with the children to measure the flour into a large bowl. Add the dried yeast. Mix these together well.

2. Add the warm water and olive oil.

3. Take turns to mix and then knead the dough in the bowl until you can gather it all together into a smooth ball.

4. Take the dough from the bowl and take turns again to knead it on the clean table top or a board until it is smooth and stretchy.

5. Put the dough back in the bowl, cover with a tea towel and put the bowl somewhere warm for 30 minutes. The dough will swell as the yeast starts to work.

6. Pull the dough into several smaller pieces, one for each child, and knead these again. Make the dough into monsters or other figures, and use the raisins to decorate them.

7. Make marks in the dough with forks or small knives. Use a garlic press to make hair.

8. Put your creations on oiled baking trays and cover with the tea towel.

9. Put the trays in a warm place and set the timer for another 30 minutes.

10. Heat the oven to 220°C/Gas Mark 8.

11. The monsters will rise under the cloth, so when the timer is done take the cloth off, and look at the monsters to talk about how they have changed.

12. Paint your monsters very gently with milk, then bake in the oven for 15-20 minutes. The bread is cooked when it sounds hollow if you tap the bottom.

✚ Health & Safety

Always supervise cooking activities carefully.

Taking it forward

- Make different types of bread – pizza dough is very easy to make and the children can decorate the pizzas with a range of toppings.

What's in it for the children?

Baking is one of the most rewarding activities for children and adults.

Top tip ⭐

While the children are waiting for the timer, Read a story together, sing some songs or have a walk outdoors.

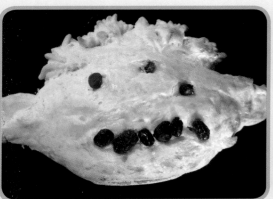

Husky dough

A different sort of dough

What you need:

- Psyllium husk powder
- An old saucepan
- A large bowl
- A cup measure and spoon
- Small bowls or plastic plates
- A whisk
- Water
- Food colouring (several colours)

Top tip ⭐

Psyllium husk is a harmless fibre supplement that you can get from a health food shop. You can use capsules, but powder is easier to manage and measure.

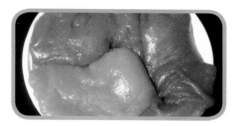

Taking it forward

- Make some brown psyllium dough and put it in a tray with dinosaurs or jungle animals.

What's in it for the children?

Any sort of dough or malleable material will exercise children's fingers and hands, and is a really good pre-writing exercise.

✚ Health & Safety

Even though this doughy slime is harmless, train the children not to eat play materials, however good they may look or smell.

What to do:

1. Put two tablespoons of psyllium husk powder in the pan. If you are using capsules, pull the capsules apart and tip out the powder into the tablespoon. Discard the empty capsules.

2. Add three cups of cold water and whisk until the powder is well mixed.

3. Add some food colouring.

4. Put the pan on a medium heat and stir all the time until the mixture bubbles, swells up and becomes transparent (adult only).

5. Remove from the heat and tip the dough out onto a plate.

6. Make some more batches of different colours.

7. Once the dough is cool, explore it. It is very stretchy and has a particular texture – it will stretch until it's almost transparent.

Note: More fibre supplement, less water gives you a more non-sticky, flubbery slime. More water and less fibre supplement gives you a more gooey sticky slime. You could try both.

Big tie dye

A collaborative tie-dye project

What you need:

- An old cotton sheet, white or a pale colour
- Elastic bands
- Plenty of buttons, marbles, beads, pebbles, small plastic toys
- Cold water dye (any colour)
- Salt
- A large bowl or bucket
- Rubber gloves and plastic aprons (child and adult sizes)

Top tip ⭐

Cotton sheets take the dye better than man-made fibres.

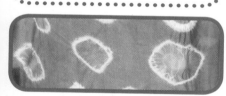

Taking it forward

- Get some sheer cotton fabric and make a tie dye parachute or smaller pieces for music and dance work.
- Use your tie dye to make curtains, table covers, or drapes for display.

What's in it for the children?

This activity is wonderful for strengthening hands and fingers, using the muscles needed later for writing. It's also a magical experience as they unwrap the objects!

➕ Health & Safety

No health and safety issues, but avoid dye splashes on clothes, carpets, etc. Dye stains won't come out.

What to do:

1. This is a long activity and it will probably take several days to get all the objects tied and to involve all the children, so find a place where they can work uninterrupted for short periods.

2. Spread out the sheet. Put an object on it, bunch the fabric to make a small parcel and wrap an elastic band tightly round the material to seal it off. You might want to demonstrate on a small piece of fabric first so that the children can see what to do (see photos).

3. Continue wrapping objects in the fabric until you've covered all of it. Keep them fairly close together. Tying objects in strings or chains gives a good effect.

4. When the sheet can't take any more objects, check the elastic bands are really tight.

5. Help the children to mix the cold water dye in the bowl, according to the instructions on the packet. Submerge the sheet and stir gently for about five minutes.

6. When the sheet has been in the dye long enough, take it out and hang it to dry a little.

7. Let the children unwrap the objects and reveal the pattern they have made together.

Come into our parlour

Pretend ice-cream play

What you need:

- Three quarters of a cup of cornflour
- Pack of gelatine
- Water
- Food colouring
- Cocoa powder
- Flavourings such as strawberry or vanilla
- Bowls, scoops, spoons and glitter for decoration

What to do:

1. Measure out the cornflour into a bowl.
2. Dissolve one packet of gelatine in one cup of hot water.
3. Quickly add this mixture to the cornflour and start mixing. Make sure there are no lumps.
4. Divide your mixture into two bowls and colour each – we used red food colouring for pink ice-cream, and cocoa powder for chocolate ice-cream. Work quickly before the gelatine sets.
5. Put the bowls in the fridge for about an hour to set.
6. Offer the ice cream for the children to play with, using scoops, spoons, little dishes, glitter etc.
7. Remind the children that it is pretend ice cream, so they cannot eat it!

Top tip ⭐

Use cocoa powder to make chocolate ice cream.

Taking it forward

- Make an ice cream parlour with the children. Ask them what they think they need and how they want to set it up.
- When the ice cream has been used in your parlour, the children can just play with it as it begins to lose its structure.

What's in it for the children?

Working together in role-play situations improves children's social skills.

✚ Health & Safety

This fake ice cream is perfectly safe to eat, but children should not be encouraged to do so – it doesn't taste very nice!